[101 WAYS TO
FLIP THE
B|RD]

JASON JOSEPH AND RICK JOSEPH

101 WAYS TO FLIP THE BIRD

Broadway Books | *New York*

PUBLISHED BY BROADWAY BOOKS

Published in the United States by Broadway Books, an imprint of
The Doubleday Broadway Publishing Group, a division of
Random House, Inc., New York.
www.broadwaybooks.com

BROADWAY BOOKS and its logo, a letter B bisected on the diagonal,
are trademarks of Random House, Inc.

Book design by Michael Collica
Illustrations by Christian Lindner: CmyWork.com

Library of Congress Cataloging-in-Publication Data

Joseph, Jason.
    101 ways to flip the bird / Jason Joseph & Rick Joseph ;
[illustration by Christian Lindner]. — 1st ed.
        p. cm.
    (alk. paper)
    1. Middle-finger gesture—Humor. I. Joseph, Rick. II. Title. III. Title: One
hundred one ways to flip the bird. IV. Title: One hundred and one ways to
flip the bird.

PN6231.026J67 2007
818'.602—dc22

                                                            2007019445

ISBN 978-0-7679-2681-2

PRINTED IN THE UNITED STATES OF AMERICA

1 3 5 7 9 10 8 6 4 2

First Edition

To our family and friends,

who remain our constant inspiration

Contents

Authors' Note

Writing this book was a lot of fun. It brought back memories of grade school, high school, college, and the last time someone cut us off in traffic. These were fun memories. Memories of giving as good as we got and getting as good as we gave. Yes, of course, we're talking about flipping the Bird.

It's part of growing up and it never really leaves you. You might be ten years old or you might be eighty; you might live in a mansion in Beverly Hills or in a trailer park in Alabama, but you can never escape the Bird. Young or old, rich or poor, we are all familiar with this hand signal, and we are neither above giving it nor most certainly above receiving it.

This book was written for those who wish to expand their skills at delivering one of our culture's most ubiquitous signs, the Bird.

Screw you all.

Sincerely,

Jason Joseph & Rick Joseph

Great Things to Say When Flipping the Bird

■ "Why don't you go play Hide and Go Screw Yourself?"

■ "Knock, Knock. [Who's there?] Screw You."

■ "Screwby-Dooby-You!"

■ "Yabba-Dabba-Screw-You!"

■ "A wise man once said, 'Screw You.'"

■ "No batter, no batter, Screw You, batter!"

■ "Ask not what your country can do for you, but Screw You."

■ "I just thought of something funny . . . Screw You."

■ "Some say the glass is half empty, some say the glass is half full, I say 'Screw You.'"

■ "Screw You and the horse you rode in on."

■ "Screw You very much."

■ "Screwidy screw screw, screwidy screw screw, screwidy screw Screw You!"

■ "Simon says 'Go Screw Yourself!'"

■ "What's the square root of Screw You?"

Warning:

Use at your own risk.

We're not responsible if

you get your ass

kicked.

[101 WAYS TO FLIP THE FLIP THE BIRD]

[I]
The Classic Flip

The originator of the "Screw You" phenomenon. It's still the easiest and most widely used. Its ease and impact make it a favorite for that split-second "Screw You" flash.

Some examples of when to use the Classic Flip are:
   a. You get cut off in traffic.
   b. A referee makes a bad call.
   c. A friend gives you a bad-hair-day comment.

Screw You How-To:

Bend your arm at the elbow joint, perpendicular to the ground. Keep your forearm vertical. Curl all your fingers into a fist while leaving your middle finger (Bird finger) extended.

The Classic Flip with Arm Cross

When a classic "Screw You" just won't do, this one has balls. The emphasis of the second hand coming across and down on the elbow joint of the giving hand makes this "Screw You" much more meaningful.

Some examples of when to use the Classic Flip with Arm Cross are:

    a. Someone drives through a puddle and splashes you on the side of the road.

    b. You lock your keys in the car.

    c. The visiting team wins against your home team on a last-second play.

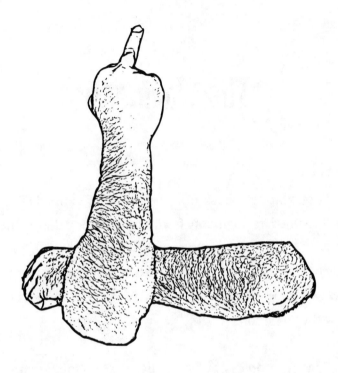

Screw You How-To:

Bend your arm at the elbow joint, perpendicular to the ground. Keep your forearm vertical. Bring your other hand across the elbow joint, keeping that arm horizontal to the ground. On the vertical hand curl all your fingers into a fist while leaving your middle finger (Bird finger) extended.

[3]
The Waving Bird

A classic brought back from the verge of extinction. It originally gained its popularity from break dancing during the '80s. Its resurgence, however, may have come around with the Michael Jackson court case, since many fans felt it was time to "wave" good-bye to the King of Pop in the same style that made him famous.

Some examples of when to use the Waving Bird are:

a. You're filled up on sushi and your brother is across the table. It's a good way to get his attention.

b. You happen to come across Michael Jackson on the street.

c. You're giving a friendly good-bye wave to a friend upon leaving a club. It adds a li'l style to your exit.

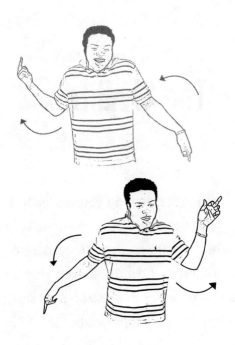

Screw You How-To:

> Starting with both arms extended, catch the "wave" motion and follow from the fingertips on one hand all the way up and down your arms to the end of the giving hand, then twist your hand around to show the Bird.

Warning: This one takes a bit of practice. Doing it wrong will really make you look like an asshole. Best to practice this one in front of a mirror and make sure you can do it smoothly.

[4]
The Sly Bird

This li'l devil is a beauty. Scratching your nose (or any part of your face) with your Bird adds a touch of style to the "Screw You." The recipient sometimes doesn't even recognize he's being "Screwed" until it's all over, and even then he's not all that sure. This one is great for more structured settings when a blatant "Screw You" is just inappropriate.

Some examples of the right time to use the Sly Bird are:

a. When you're at a dinner party and one of the guests pisses you off.

b. This is the perfect "Screw You" to the teacher from the back of the class. If it's done quickly enough you can get away with it. Be careful and don't linger here.

c. When a friend makes a sly smart-ass comment to you.

Screw You How-To:

   Use your Bird to scratch a part of your face.

[5]
The Draw

A "Screw You" with a Wild West flavor. Legend has it Doc Holliday once used the Draw on a guy in the street and the guy dropped dead of a heart attack. Talk about a powerful "Screw You." Of course, it's only a legend, so don't be afraid of using this one on your friends.

Some examples of the appropriate time to use the Draw are:

a. When you see a good friend in the middle of the hall, especially if he's carrying a lot of books.

b. Whenever you're in Arizona, Nevada, Utah, etc.

c. On Halloween when you see someone dressed as a cowboy—or whenever you see someone in one of those "urban cowboy" hats.

Screw You How-To:

Pretend you're pulling your Bird from your hip like a gun from a holster.

Warning: Never, I repeat, never use this one on a police officer or a gang member, as they have real guns.

[6]
The Double Draw

Same as the Draw, only you bring both hands into the act. If you're a real asshole this one will let people know you mean business. After all, two have twice the impact of one. To really add insult to the "Screw You," blow on your finger tips before holstering your Birds. It lets people know you definitely "Screwed" them.

Some examples of great times to use the Double Draw are:
   a. While you're watching a Clint Eastwood western with your friends.
   b. When you're leaving Arizona, Nevada, Utah, etc.
   c. On Halloween when YOU'RE dressed as a cowboy.

Screw You How-To:

Pull both Birds from your hips, pretending they are guns being pulled from holsters.

Warning: Remember, don't mess with people who carry guns.

Gotcha

This is great for the prankster in all of us. It's very personal and is great to use on the guys who are dressed to impress. You'll be the one impressing the ladies when you "Screw You" to Lou. Assuming Lou doesn't have a short fuse and kick your ass.

Some good times to use Gotcha are:

a. When your friend is overdressed at a nightclub.
b. When someone really has something on their shirt.
c. When your friend is wearing an ugly tie.

Screw You How-To:

Simply touch your Bird against his chest and tell him he has something on his shirt. When he looks down, bring your Bird up and glance it off his chin.

[8]
Windshield Wipers

A little cheesy, but under the right circumstances it can be effective. Save this one for a rainy day, literally.

Examples of when to use Windshield Wipers are:
   a. In the passenger seat of your friend's car when it starts to rain.
   b. You're walking outside in the cold and your friend's glasses fog up.
   c. While you're looking out a dirty window.

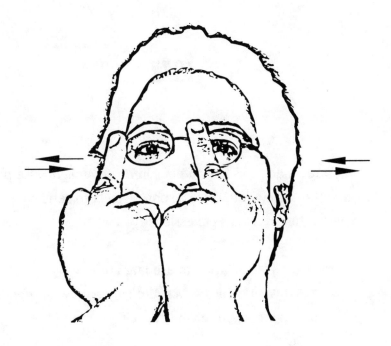

Screw You How-To:

Starting with both hands out and your Birds horizontal to the floor pointing in, simply rotate both 90 degrees away from each other at the wrist so they are parallel to each other and pointing straight up. Next, bring them back to the starting position. Repeat several times.

[9]
Jazz

Jim Carrey made this one famous in *Bruce Almighty*. He perfected the "Screw You" there, so don't expect to perform quite as well as he did. He's a professional, you're not.

Some examples of when to use Jazz are:

    a. While watching *Bruce Almighty* with your friends.

    b. In a record store while walking through the jazz section.

    c. Just before you change the radio station in the car when a jazz song comes on.

Screw You How-To:

Ask your target if he likes jazz. Then proceed to put both
hands up to your mouth, mimicking playing a sax or
trumpet. Remember to look sideways at your target. Blow
into your fingers and flip the Bird on a high note.

The Poltergeist

So named after the 1982 Steven Spielberg movie in which it first appeared. This Bird was popular for a short time but it quickly faded. Its similarities to the Macarena and the Jeannie can make it a bit confusing.

Some suggestions for when to use the Poltergeist are:
a. While watching *Poltergeist*, of course.
b. Some jerk makes a rude sexual comment to you.
c. You're flipping off a ghost or a spirit.

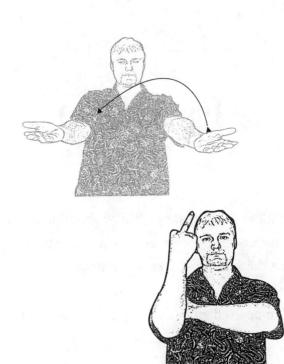

Screw You How-To:

Stand facing your target and extend both hands palms up. Next, raise your left forearm up in the air from the elbow. That arm falls down over the right elbow joint, driving the right forearm up to become the giving hand and turning this into the Classic Flip with Arm Cross.

The Macarena

Yes, that dumb-ass song they still play at weddings. This "Screw You" is never cool. However, if you get stuck doing the Macarena this may make it easier to stomach.

ONLY to be used while actually doing the Macarena.

Screw You How-To:

> After you've completed the steps to the song itself, and your hands are on your hips, simply turn it into a Classic Flip. Just remember not to hold it there; continue with the rest of the stupid-ass song/dance and pray no one is making a video. (Lots of luck, sucker.)

The Jeannie

Similar to both the Poltergeist and the Macarena, this Bird is more widely accepted among the baby-boomer generation. It originated with the *I Dream of Jeannie* show that's on Nick at Nite now. May gain Generation X status once the movie version comes out later this decade. This oldie but goodie basically says "Your wish is my 'Screw You.' "

Some good examples of when to use the Jeannie are:

    a. You're standing in line waiting to buy tickets for the movie version of *I Dream of Jeannie* and someone cuts in front of you.

    b. You come across a girl named Jeannie. Of course, this may not be the best way to break the ice.

    c. A dumb-ass friend says, "I wish . . . "

Screw You How-To:

Stand straight, cross both arms in front of you, give a
little head nod and blink, then raise your right arm into
the Classic Flip with Arm Cross.

13

The Glasses Adjuster
(aka the Clark Kent)

This not-so-subtle "Screw You" is great in an office setting. Can be used only if you wear glasses (sunglasses work, too).

Some examples of when to use the Glasses Adjuster are:

a. During a business meeting when someone interrupts you.

b. Any situation that involves Superman.

c. You're on the beach and a dorky guy hits on you. This destroys his self-esteem for years to come.

Screw You How-To:

Push your glasses back up tight to your face over the rim of your nose using your Bird. The slower the better.

14

Read Between the Lines

Simple yet very effective. This Bird forces the receiver to do a little thinking before he realizes he's being "Screwed." It's one that never goes out of style. It may, however, be overused by some people. If this is the case, please give them a copy of this book so they can get some variety. Thank you.

Some good times to use Read Between the Lines are:
    a. In an educational setting such as a high school or college.
    b. In a quiet place such as a library or church.
    c. During a book club meeting when someone speaks out of turn.

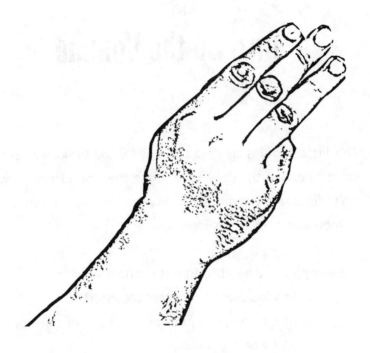

Screw You How-To:

> Extend the Bird finger along with the index and ring fingers together. While doing this Classic Flip motion say, "Read between the lines."

15

Turn Up the Volume

This little doozy is creative and not for the timid. It uses sarcasm to enrich the delivery. If you're the kind of person who isn't afraid to tell someone "Screw You" in no uncertain terms to their face, then this is for you.

Examples of when this Bird is useful are:
a. In a loud setting such as a concert.
b. At a bar when a guy you don't like hits on you and won't go away.
c. In school in front of your friends to really belittle your victim, sending him into therapy.

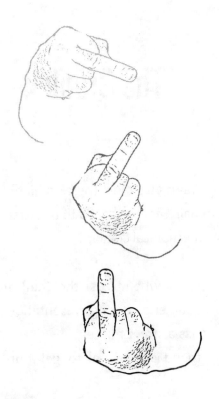

Screw You How-To:

When facing your victim, extend your arm and flip the Bird downward (upside-down Classic Flip). Ask the target if he can hear you and say, "Then let me turn up the volume," at which point you rotate your wrist upward to the Classic Flip position.

16

The Crank

This one really draws attention. There's a hint of showboating with a touch of flair. Engineers tend to be attracted to this one as it imitates a mechanical crank.

Some examples of when to use the Crank are:
a. During an engineering presentation.
b. You pass a street mime.
c. Your friend is too drunk to "get it up."

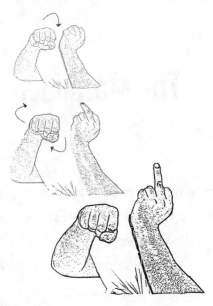

Screw You How-To:

    Raise your left arm in the standard 90-degree position bent at the elbow, but keep your hand in a loose fist. Take your right hand and simulate a cranking motion as if an imaginary handle was sticking out of your left hand. While cranking, slowly raise the Bird on your left hand till it's completely erect, hold, then reverse the cranking motion while slowly lowering your Bird back to the starting point.

    Sound effects optional.

17

The Marauder

Named after the mascot of the high school where it was first introduced. This one is tricky and takes some coordination and skill. Please practice while your car is parked, as preventing traffic accidents will also prevent you from being the recipient of a Classic Flip.

Some great times to use the Marauder are:

a. If you go to a high school that has a Marauder as its mascot.

b. If you're on a varsity team and you see JV or underclassmen walking near the school.

c. When it's 95 degrees, in the middle of summer, you're in a convertible, and you see someone you know looking for a ride to the store to get a cold drink.

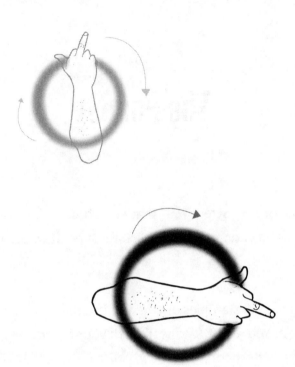

Screw You How-To:

> At about the nine-o'clock position on the steering wheel, with your right hand, grip the wheel from underneath, palm up. While making a right turn, extend your Bird only and slowly proceed through the turn. Getting the attention of your prey can be accomplished with a quick beep of the horn or a shout out of the window.

18

The Pointer

Another classic "Screw You" that sometimes goes unnoticed. It's a misdirection marvel. The Pointer is great to use on slow people.

Some good examples of when to use the Pointer are:
a. You're out for a walk with your friends on a sunny afternoon.
b. In response to a dork asking directions.
c. You're pointing out something in the sky (a cloud, a bird, a flying saucer, etc.).

Screw You How-To:

Point out an object with your Bird instead of your index finger.

19

Here, I've Got Something for You

Fantastic "Screw You" to friends who are always broke and mooching off of you. This pocket buddy is worth the price of admission the first time it's used on an unsuspecting leech. The look of expectation that quickly turns into disappointment and sometimes embarrassment is priceless.

Best times to use this one are:

    a. When your cheap-ass friend asks to borrow money—again.

    b. If you're a big ass yourself, you can use this on people collecting for charities. Not recommended unless you know the person.

    c. If your balls itch, it makes a great cover for scratching them.

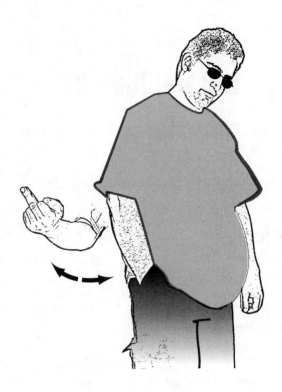

Screw You How-To:

> While reaching into your pockets simply say, "Here, I've got something for you," and pull out the Bird and turn it into a Classic Flip. You can even add a little more spice by saying "Keep the change."

20

The Double Cox

So named after Bryan Cox, the infamous Miami Dolphins football player who came into Buffalo flipping both Birds at the fans and was caught on camera. It used to have many other names: the Double Flip, the Double Classic Flip, the infamous Screw You All. However, when a loser named Cox does it on national television and gets fined thousands of dollars, he essentially buys the naming rights.

Some examples of when to use the Double Cox are:
   a. If you're a Cox.
   b. NOT in front of a television camera.
   c. If NFL fans throw batteries at you on the sideline (because you Double Coxed them already).

Screw You How-To:

Give the Classic Flip with both arms stretched above your head.

21

The Sneak Attack

(aka the Behind the Back Attack)

For the wimp in all of us that just can't face up to telling some-one "Screw You" to their face. This one is for when you're afraid to face the consequences of your Bird, so you wait till the recip-ient is turned around with his back to you. Although done out of sight, this does not make it exclusively for wussies. In fact, if done in front of an audience against an authority figure, it's quite powerful.

Some examples of times to use the Sneak Attack are:
   a. In a classroom setting when the teacher isn't looking.
   b. After a police officer gives you a ticket or warning. (Make damn sure he doesn't see you do it, or it can lead to a world of trouble.)
   c. When a bigger guy insults you and then turns away.

Screw You How-To:

Wait till the person you want to "Screw" turns around or looks away, then flip him the Bird.

[22]
The Sit-'n'-Spin

For graphic and vulgar individuals who like to really lay on the details. Describing what your recipient can really do with your Bird is downright disgusting. A word of advice: if they actually WANT to take you up on your offer . . . RUN!!!

Some examples of when to and when *not* to use this one are:
   a. Your boss really pisses you off and you quit.
   b. NEVER use this if you're a proctologist. Totally unprofessional.

Screw You How-To:

Use the Classic Flip and add words like "Why don't you sit-'n'-spin on this?" or "Shove this up your . . . " or the classic "Shove this where the sun don't shine."

The Tea Bird

No, not the car. This one comes from our friends the Brits. The English love tea and are very proper, polite, and almost ritualistic when they drink it. When an Englishman is drinking tea his pinky finger sticks out. This, of course, annoys the hell out of everyone else.

Some good times to use the Tea Bird are:

  a. If you're a member of the English royal family and you see some paparazzi.

  b. While watching a soccer game.

  c. At the prom.

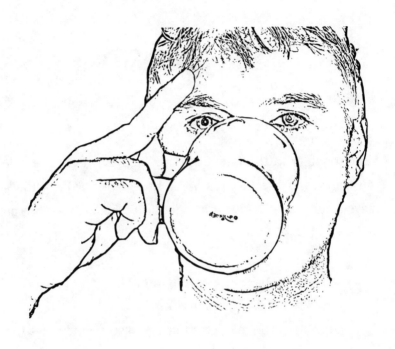

Screw You How-To:

> When drinking tea, or any drink really, stick out your Bird instead of your pinky.

[24]

The Egyptian

Made popular in the late '80s/early '90s by the hot female musical group the Bangles. At a time when MTV actually played music and had music videos, this beauty became an instant cult classic.

Some times to use the Egyptian are:
   a. When a Bangles song comes on.
   b. When you're in Egypt or when somebody says the word "Egypt."
   c. When somebody asks you your nationality and you tell them you're Egyptian.

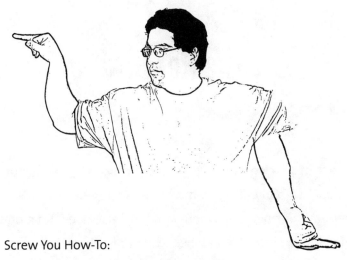

Screw You How-To:

 While posing to walk like an Egyptian, have one foot in front of the other. One arm is up, parallel to the floor and bent 90 degrees at the elbow upward. The wrist is actually bent forward so that your hand is palm down, parallel to the floor. It is here that you give the Bird, but remember to keep it horizontal. Your other arm is behind you, parallel to the floor and bent 90 degrees at the elbow downward. The wrist is bent backward as your hand is palm up, parallel to the floor. Again, here you give the Bird while keeping it horizontal. As you "walk like an Egyptian," switch your arm positions in a fluid motion.

25

The Pet Bird

The act of petting our dogs or cats brings us joy. A lot of us actually use baby talk when we are petting our pet. It's cute when it's your pet, but when someone else does it it's pretty lame. So here's the deal; when you're at a baby-talk petter's house and you have the chance to pet their pet, this beauty is priceless. It can be hard to detect because the fur makes a good concealer/cover.

Some good examples of when to use the Pet Bird are:
    a. At your friend's house, petting his dog, while you wait patiently for his slow ass to get ready.
    b. You're visiting old people who push their precious lap dog on your lap when you're just trying to be nice.
    c. You're petting your own dog while watching TV.

Screw You How-To:

  While petting an animal, keep your Bird extended the
  whole time and "pet" with the backs/knuckles of your
  other fingers.

26

The Conductor

For the music lover, or hater, in all of us. The better you are dressed the better this works. If you can find an opportunity to wear a tuxedo with tails, you, my man, are as ready as it gets.

Some great examples of when to use the Conductor are:
a. At a wedding reception where you are the best man.
b. In the back of the opera house while you are returning to your seat from your much-needed bathroom break.
c. Your friend is having wild sex in the next room and you can hear them through the walls.

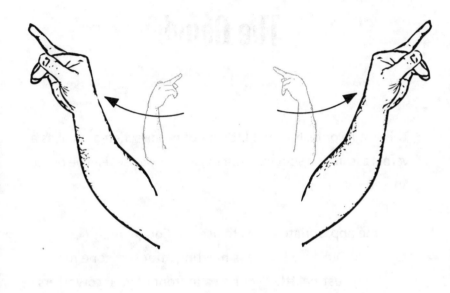

Screw You How-To:

Just like the conductor of a symphony who uses his baton to direct the music, use your two Birds to direct the music.

[27]
The Cough

This is a favorite. It uses a little bit of misdirection as well as a verbal assault on your victim. It's also a very close relative of the Sneeze.

Some appropriate times to use the Cough are:
  a. During a business meeting after someone has just belittled your idea in front of your coworkers.
  b. When someone has just told a joke at your expense.
  c. When an inconsiderate smoker blows smoke in your face.

Screw You How-To:

While faking a cough, simply cover your mouth with your fist leaving your Bird exposed. Make sure that your fake cough comes out sounding like "Screw You."

28

The Sneeze

As mentioned before, a close relative of the Cough. It is used basically the same way; a bit of misdirection and a verbal assault.

Some good times to use the Sneeze are:

a. If you're allergic to cats and your friend who has a cat knows this and allows her cat to rub against your leg repeatedly.

b. When you're outside playing basketball with your friends and one of them fouls you and says something stupid like "Playground rules."

c. When you're having dinner with your family and your sister tells your parents a secret about what you do in the bathroom for so long.

Screw You How-To:

> While faking a sneeze, cover your nose and mouth with
> one or both hands, palms facing you, while leaving the
> Bird (or both Birds) sticking out. Make the sneeze sound
> like "Screw You."

29

The Salute

For those of us with a military background or mind-set. When following orders from the idiot in charge is just too damn stressful, this "Screw You" works out nicely.

Some examples of when to use the Salute are:

a. To your drill sergeant on the last day you have to put up with basic training. (Using the Follow Through on this one as a blatant "Screw You" is still rather dangerous.)

b. Your friend comes home from the service.

c. You meet a skinhead dressed in paramilitary attire. (Of course if you're stupid enough to do this to one of those guys, you better be able to handle yourself quite well or you WILL get your ass kicked).

Screw You How-To:

There are two ways to do this one, depending on what type of situation you are in. If complete lack of respect is called for, then the Entire Salute should be applied. However, if you don't want to get thrown in the brig, then the Follow Through salute should be implemented.

- For the Entire Salute, bring your right hand up toward your forehead and hold it there with your Bird sticking out and your other fingers closed. (Blatant disrespect.)
- The Follow Through is a normal Salute, but as your hand comes back down close your hand in a fist keeping your Bird exposed. (Less obvious and safer.)

30

The Screwball

This tasteless and disrespectful "Screw You" is actually a cover. Ninety-nine percent of the time a person uses it to scratch their balls. The other 1 percent it's just used to scratch the head.

Appropriate times to use the Screwball are:

    a. When your balls itch.

    b. When your head itches.

    c. When your balls AND head itch.

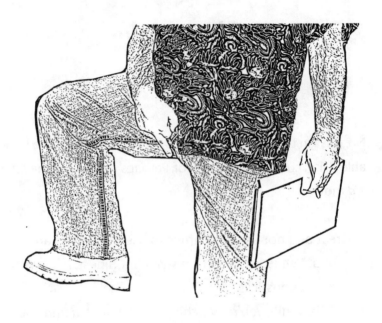

Screw You How-To:

Scratch your balls but keep your Bird out. To cover your intentions, make sure you tell your target "Screw You" or "Right Here."

31

Chopsticks

No, this isn't the piano song. This comes to us from the honorable Asian cultures. Well, kind of. Perhaps more from the *Karate Kid* movies.

Great and not-so-great times to use Chopsticks are:

a. While you're eating sushi or Chinese food with chopsticks.

b. While you're watching *The Karate Kid* and you grab a pair of chopsticks and try to catch a fly with them like in the movie. Of course if someone is with you he has every right to use any other Bird on you for doing this.

c. If you're on vacation in Japan, show some respect and use the chopsticks without using Chopsticks.

Screw You How-To:

While using chopsticks, extend your Bird.

32

The Thinker
(aka Rodin's Thinker)

For the cultured and art connoisseurs out there who actually know who Auguste Rodin was. For the rest of you uneducated dumb asses, he was an artist born in the mid-1800s in Paris. His work *The Thinker* is one of the most replicated sculptures in history. It's a sculpture of a man in a seated position with his chin resting on his right fist.

Some examples of when to use the Thinker are:
  a. At a museum during a tour.
  b. While you're on the toilet going Number 2.
  c. While you're leaning in close to someone, pretending you want to hear more of their boring crap.

Screw You How-To:

    While in a seated position with your chin resting on your right fist, raise your Bird.

33

Sorry, I'm Deaf

For the hard of hearing or when you're trying to ignore somebody. It's most often used on one's nagging spouse. This works really well for anyone, but it's perfect for the senior citizen with a mean streak. This is the "Screw You" of the old folks' home.

Good examples of when to use Sorry, I'm Deaf are:
   a. If you're actually deaf or hard of hearing.
   b. Your wife keeps nagging you to do something, over and over, with no end in sight other than the final relief of a welcome heart attack.
   c. Your friends are whispering something to each other that is most likely about you and you can almost hear them.

Screw You How-To:

   When someone is talking to you, pretend like you can't
   hear them and put your hand, cupped, behind your ear.
   Cup all your fingers except your Bird, keeping it straight
   up.

[34]
Hit Me
(aka Blackjack)

If you're a gambler, then there's no doubt you've played black-jack at a casino. And as anyone knows, losing money isn't fun. If you're sick of constantly busting, this "Screw You" was made for you, ya loser. If losing all your money isn't enough for you, using this too blatantly can get you kicked out of the casino and even banned, so be discreet.

Examples of proper times to use Hit Me are:
   a. When you're getting your butt handed to you at the blackjack table at the casino.
   b. While playing BJ on the video machine at the casino, and losing big.
   c. At a stag party and you're playing BJ before the entertainment gets there.

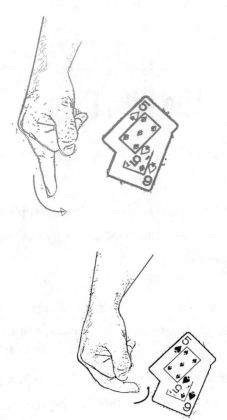

Screw You How-To:

When it comes time at the BJ table for you to let the
dealer know if you want another card ("Hit me"), instead
of using your index and Bird fingers together to show
this, use only your Bird.

[35]
The Bird Clap

For sophisticated and classy types, like those people who like to go to the opera. It's basically used either by the stuck-up and arrogant or against them.

Appropriate times to use the Bird Clap are:
a. During a debate when the speaker finishes his or her argument.
b. When a kid peels out to show off in his expensive new sports car his daddy just bought for him.
c. At the opera.

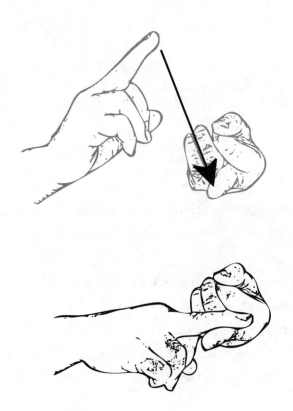

Screw You How-To:

Rather than clap with two open palms, clap your two Birds together.

36

The Pick

A rather disgusting "Screw You." If you want to gross a person out AND "Screw" them, this baby is for you.

Good times to use the Pick are:

    a. If you're trailer-park trash.

    b. If you're a nerd.

    c. If your favorite movie character is Booger from *Revenge of the Nerds*.

Screw You How-To:

Pick your nose with your Bird. (Remember to wash your hands afterward, you filthy pig.)

37

The Nipple Rub

Considered erotic till fat guys started using it after seeing the *Austin Powers* movies. Little known fact: this Bird used to be known as Twin Peaks, but apparently not everyone's nipples become erect while doing it.

Examples of when one might use the Nipple Rub are:
 a. If you're a hot chick, it's always in fashion.
 b. You see a hot girl with a T.H.O. (Tittie Hard-on).
 c. You have nipple piercings and someone makes a comment about them.

Screw You How-To:

Rub your Birds in circles around your nipples. May include a pre-rub lick to the tips of your Birds.

38

The Archer

Believe it or not, one theory of where flipping the Bird originated comes from English archers giving the French the "bird"
after a battle. At the time, the "bird" was the finger used to
draw back the bowstring in order to shoot the arrows. So
we respectfully pay homage with this imitation.

Good times to use the Archer are:
   a. If you find yourself in France.
   b. While making fun of a friend who's in love, use
      this bird and say he's hit with Cupid's arrow.
   c. If you are a bow hunter and people piss you off.

Screw You How-To:

Pretending to draw back a bow and arrow, keep your Bird closed in the fist till you release the arrow at your target by extending it.

39

The Rifle

(aka the Scope)

Based on the Archer, this "Screw You" zeros in on its intended target. Once he's lined up in your sights, you can really nail the loser.

Examples of times to use the Rifle are:

    a. During rabbit season.

    b. During duck season.

    c. While watching Bugs Bunny and Daffy Duck cartoons.

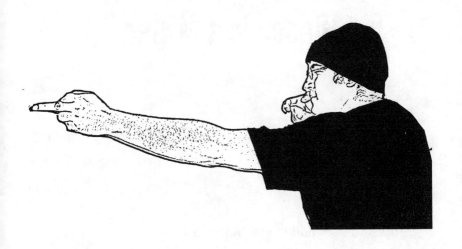

Screw You How-To:

Pretend you are holding a gun. Keep your left arm out and your right arm up with the base of your thumb touching your right eye. Keep your trigger finger out till you pull the trigger, at which point the Bird on your left hand shoots out.

40

Hidden in a Mitten

Used primarily in colder climates. Can only be done while actually wearing mittens. It's as close to concealed as possible, yet its intent is obvious.

Times to use Hidden in a Mitten are:

    a. On the ski slopes.

    b. Outdoors when it's too damn cold to take off your mittens to "Screw" someone.

    c. At a football game when you're bundled up for the cold and the other team has just benefited from a bad call by the referee.

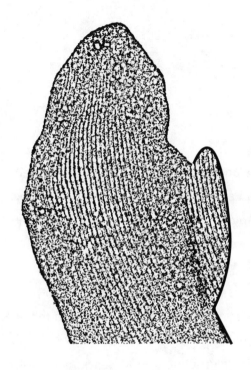

Screw You How-To:

    While wearing mittens, give someone the Classic Flip.

[41]
The Runner

For people who are literally on the run. This "Screw You" moves so fast sometimes only your subconscious or a slow motion video replay can pick it up. It's believed to give a runner a sense of power that results in faster runs.

Relevant times to use the Runner are:
   a. While you're running in the Boston marathon, if you're from New York City.
   b. At those grueling double sessions in high school football when you have to get in shape by running laps around the track.
   c. When a really big guy you just insulted is chasing your ass.

Screw You How-To:

> While running, instead of keeping your hands in loose
> fists or open all the way, keep all your fingers closed
> except your Birds, which are held erect.

42

The Laborer

(aka the Workhorse)

Manual labor sucks. It's hard and backbreaking, and some-times, no matter what you do, it's not good enough for your incompetent managers or front office. Since you're at the bottom of the totem pole, all you can do is take it when they give it and smile. Well, this "Screw You" helps relieve a little bit of the stress and tension.

Examples of when to use the Laborer are:
   a. Management's decisions have cost the company's stockholders millions of dollars and hundreds are being laid off, and they always end up blaming it all on the laborer.
   b. You feel like the harder you work and the more you follow company rules, the more they single you out and screw you, because they can.

Screw You How-To:

> While carrying something that is thrown over your shoulder, keep the Bird up on your hand that holds it down. It works great on objects such as ladders, pipes, hoses, etc.

43

Captain Says "Screw You"

(Even-Odds)

At some point in their life everyone has played the even-odds game. You know the game where two or more people pick evens or odds and then everyone puts one hand behind their back? You face each other and when the person calling the game says, "Captain says 'Shoot,'" you pull your hand out in front of you holding up a certain number of fingers. You add the total number of fingers everyone is holding up and see if it's odd or even, thus deciding the winner. Simple math. It's a little corny for a "Screw You," but you have to take what you can get when you can get it.

There's really only one time to use this:

> a. When you're playing Even-Odds (sometimes known as Captain Says "Shoot").

Screw You How-To:

>   Face your recipient, put your hand behind your back, and
>   when you hear "Captain says 'Shoot,'" just come out and
>   give the Bird when you bring your hand back in front of
>   you.

*Bonus Screw: If you're the one calling the game, instead of saying
"Captain says 'Shoot,'" say "Captain says 'Screw You.'"*

[44]

Rock, Paper, Screw You

A more advanced game than Even-Odds, the basics of the game are the same. Rock beats scissors, scissors beat paper, and paper beats rock. Only instead of scissors it's "Screw You."

Appropriate times to use Rock, Paper, Screw You are:
   a. While playing Rock, Paper, Scissors, of course, you moron.
   b. See above example, nitwit.
   c. Are you actually still looking for another example of when to use this?

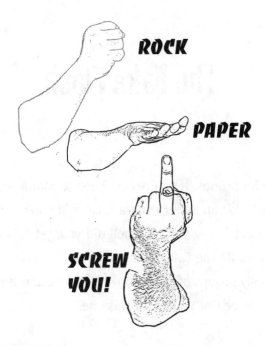

ROCK

PAPER

SCREW YOU!

Screw You How-To:

> Hand in a fist represents rock. Hand open flat represents paper. Index and Bird fingers used to represent scissors, but now ONLY Bird represents "Screw You."

> Bend your elbow and have your hand vertical to the ground. Count down ("Three . . . two . . . one . . . "). Bring your hand down to a horizontal position and instead of showing rock, paper, or scissors, flip the Bird.

45

The Fake Flash

A favorite for prudes. If you've ever been to Mardi Gras or seen *Girls Gone Wild* you know what a Flash is. If you're so innocent and you don't know, why the hell did you get this book, you poor naïve soul? The Fake Flash *really*, *really*, *really* pisses guys off, especially groups of guys drinking large quantities of alcohol, so ladies, be CAREFUL with this one.

Best times to use the Fake Flash are:
   a. At Mardi Gras, IF AND ONLY IF you are on a balcony and the horde of drunken testosterone can't reach you.
   b. You're at a party and your guy friends are daring you to flash them.
   c. In a hot-body contest at a bar and the crowd starts chanting "Skin to win."

Screw You How-To:

Pretend that you are about to take off your shirt or pull it
up to expose your breasts, release the shirt so it falls back
down at the last possible moment, and give the guys a
Double Cox (refer to #20 for more info).

46

The Jerk Off

For the immature, or immature at heart, a "Screw You" based on "Screwing Yourself." Since your sex life is nonexistent, you might as well use your expertise in self-love (yank, yank) as a tool to put others down.

Fun times to Jerk Off are:

     a. Home alone.

     b. In the shower.

     c. When someone asks what you did last night.

Screw You How-To:

> Guys, you don't need directions for this, just know that
> it's done in public OVER your pants with your Bird out—
> not, I repeat, *not* your penis. (Or, occasionally, from behind
> a shower curtain, as pictured above.)

47

Three . . . Two . . . One . . .

When done right, this beauty gets great laughs, albeit from simpleminded folk. It's best used when someone is on camera, whether in a home movie, on the news, or just in a picture. It's priceless if you can get the surprised reaction on tape or in a picture, which will last forever.

Pretty funny times to use Three . . . Two . . . One . . . are:

a. While taking a family picture where you are the photographer and you want to get a great reaction picture.

b. If you work behind the camera in the newsroom and your job is to let the newscasters know when they are about to come back on the air live.

c. As a good countdown to a loud fart.

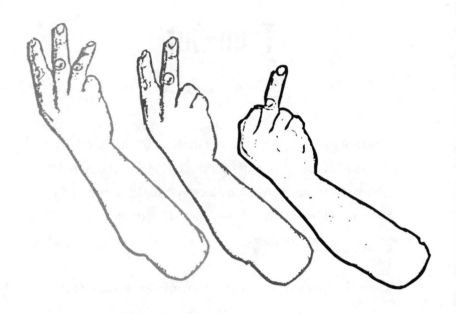

Screw You How-To:

> While counting down to something, such as when you're preparing to take a picture, say the words "Three . . . Two . . . One . . ." and simultaneously use your fingers. Three middle fingers, V sign with index and Bird, and, of course, numero uno: the Bird.

48

Time-Out

This "Screw You" is for the sports fanatics out there. When the cheesehead in your group of friends starts to melt down while watching a Packers game, this looney tune deserves a Time-Out. Or an intervention. Either way, something needs to be done to calm the situation.

Some examples of when to give someone a Time-Out are:

a. You're playing football and your initials are T.O. (as in Terrell Owens) and you need to get a ref's attention, this will work.

b. Your friend's drunk little brother is freaking in the parking lot of the stadium after his team just lost.

c. Someone's talking too fast for you to hear because you're drunk.

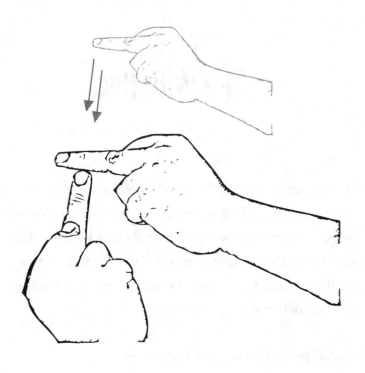

Screw You How-To:

When you call a T.O. in sports, you bring the palm of your left hand across and down over the tips of the fingers on your right to form a "T." For this Bird, close the rest of your fingers on both hands and touch your Birds perpendicular to each other.

49

The Whistler

You ain't just whistling "Dixie." If you have no idea what that means then I'm getting old or you're too young. If you're able to use your fingers in your mouth to make that really loud annoying whistle, then this "Screw You" was made specifically for you. It's basically for people who really want to get someone's attention before they "Screw" them.

Good times to use the Whistler are:

a. At a sporting event during a time-out or lull in the action when it's quiet so the referee or the opposing team's players can really hear you and turn to see you "Screw" them.

b. If you trained your dog to come when you whistle and that damn thing just ran off again chasing a car.

Screw You How-To:

Insert the Bird from each hand in your mouth and use
them to produce a loud whistle.

[50]
The Playboy
(aka the Hugh Hefner)

This is the only way to flip the Bird without ever giving the finger. If you reach a point in life where you are sooo successful and admired by women, you don't ever have to tell someone "Screw You." Walking around with two or more HOT women on your arms is the best way to tell someone "Screw You."

Best times to use the Playboy are:

    a. If you're lucky enough to be invited to the Playboy Mansion for a party, that's a "Screw You" to the rest of us poor souls who will never have that dream come true. That, my friend, lasts a lifetime.

    b. If you're the one and only Hugh Hefner, Mr. Playboy.

    c. If you're a professional athlete or you just won the lottery.

Screw You How-To:

Become rich and famous to the point that you can have any woman you want and live life to the fullest. Enjoy the spoils of your success and just walk around with complete confidence.

A smoking pipe and pajamas provide added flair.

51

The Flicker Screw

Sometimes M&M's, Tic Tacs, Jolly Ranchers, or other small edible objects make great ammo for flicking across the room to get someone's attention. Now you can bypass the ammo and flick them directly with your Bird.

Good times to use the Flicker Screw:

    a. In the cafeteria while sitting at a table with your friends and one of them isn't laughing at your jokes.

    b. When a bug is crawling on your desk.

    c. When you want to flick someone's ear when you're behind them in line.

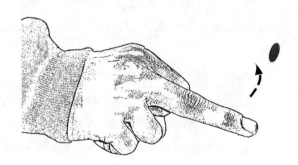

Screw You How-To:

Use your Bird to flick a small object at someone and keep it out once you've got your target's attention.

52

The OK

One of the most commonly used hand signs when everything is OK. It's just as popular as the thumbs-up sign signaling everything is fine. Well, this OK just says "OK, Screw You."

Good examples of when it's okay to use the OK are:

    a. You're playing a game and the ball bounces up and hits you right in the balls and you keel over and one of your dumb-ass friends comes up and asks if you're all right.

    b. Someone with less experience than you is showing you how to do the thing that you're an expert at.

    c. Some moron states his opinion on politics and is so off-base you almost die laughing.

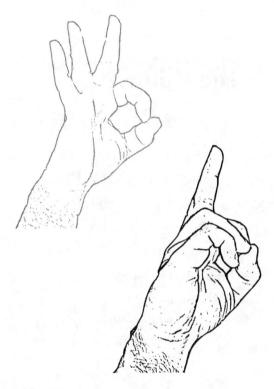

Screw You How-To:

    To start, make the popular OK sign with your thumb and index finger tips touching to form an "O," and the other three fingers raised and fanned out creating a look of a "K." Instead of keeping all three fingers up, just keep your Bird up and curl the others into a fist.

[53]
The Rubber Band

Very similar to the Flicker Screw. This fun "Screw You" can really hurt your target if you have good aim.

Use the Rubber Band when:
   a. Your friend isn't looking.
   b. He has his hands full.
   c. He's talking to the prettiest girl in school in the hallway.

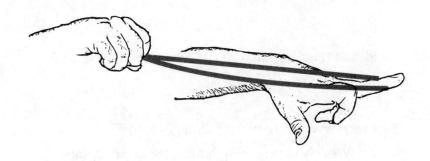

Screw You How-To:

Pull back a rubber band with your right hand and use the
Bird of your left hand to aim. Release.

54

The Dragger

If the idea of touching what you're "Screwing" appeals to you, then this is definitely your baby.

Examples of when to use the Dragger are:

a. While you're reading Braille, say, on something stupid like a drive-up ATM.

b. You see a car parked that's really dirty, so you write "wash me" on it in the dirt with your Bird.

c. You're a drill sergeant and doing a white-glove inspection.

Screw You How-To:

Use your Bird and drag it along an object for any length of time or space.

55

Shhhh

Mothers are *sooooooo* tempted to use this one when their kids are being loud again in public. Yes, moms have more restraint than the rest of us, but don't let that stop you—rock on!

Common examples of when to use Shhhh are:

a. Your friends are arguing again and you want them to quiet down.

b. You're a mother who's had it and is about to lose it.

c. People are talking loudly in the movie theater behind you during the movie.

Screw You How-To:

Make the *shhhh* sign of putting your finger against your lips and making the sound "*shhhh*," only this time use your Bird.

[56]

The Unconscious

It's the things that we do unconsciously that are the funniest, because we do them without thinking about the consequences. The Unconscious can be any Bird; it's defined by when you use it.

Examples of when we use the Unconscious are:
  a. You're trying to sleep and a friend is trying to annoy you.
  b. Someone just made a great put-down at your expense in front of your friends.
  c. You almost get in an accident after someone cuts you off in traffic. It's basically impossible not to flip the Bird when this happens.

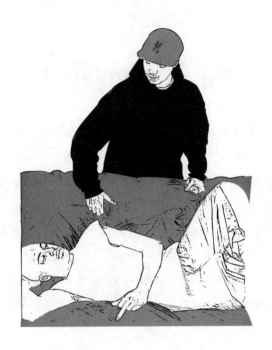

Screw You How-To:

    Give the Bird as a knee-jerk reaction without even think-

    ing about it.

57

The Cowboy Belt

So named for the rednecks—sorry, "cowboys"—who wear big belt buckles and use them as a hand rest. You know that cool cowboy stance, leaning against a wall smoking a Marlboro with one hand and resting the other in their pants right at the belt. If not, just watch any country-western video and there's a great chance you'll see it.

Some examples of when to use the Cowboy Belt are:

a. You're a redneck.

b. While waiting in line for your food stamps.

c. You think no one knows you're bald under your cowboy hat.

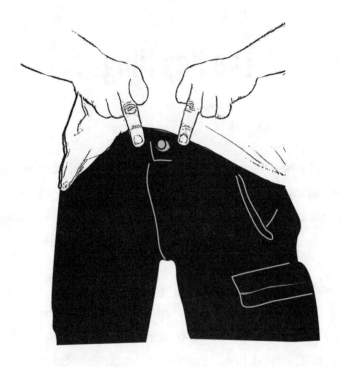

Screw You How-To:

Tuck your thumbs into your waistband leaving your Birds
pointing down.

58

The Key Ring

Best used when you're the driver. Are you sick of your friends always calling "shotgun" when you step outside so they get the front seat of the car before anyone else? Then this is a sweet one.

Good times to use the Key Ring are:

   a. When you're the designated driver and your friends want to go to another bar.
   b. The next time someone calls out "shotgun."
   c. When you just got a new car and want to show it off.

Screw You How-To:

Pull your keys out and twirl them on your Bird and say
"Screw You, I'm the driver."

59

The Shut-Up Flash

Almost an Unconscious flash but you put a little more thought into it. When you're sick of someone's lip or something that is making a lot of noise, this "Screw You" is perfect.

Use the Shut-Up Flash when:

    a. You get home and your neighbor's dog is barking at you, all the way from your car to your front door.

    b. Someone of less importance than you is trying to talk to you, like, say, you're a senior and a freshman is talking to you.

    c. You are about to quit your job and your supervisor is trying to talk down to you. Also helps to add, "Screw You, I quit!"

Screw You How-To:

> While walking away or turned away from your target,
> wave your arm toward them as if you're dismissing them,
> only keep your Bird up and the rest of your fingers down.

60

The Snapper

Attention-getter, cool, stylish, all the things you're not. But it's OK, you can still use this "Screw You"— it's a snap, literally.

Snappy times to use the Snapper are:

    a. When your friends are all talking at the table and you're trying to get their attention.

    b. If you don't know how to whistle to get attention, this is the next best thing.

    c. While eating a Slim Jim. Snap into it.

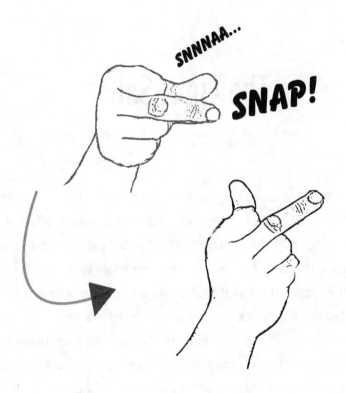

SNNNAA...

SNAP!

Screw You How-To:

>Instead of snapping your thumb against your Bird finger, snap your thumb against your index finger while keeping your Bird up.

61

The Light Saber

Use the Force, Luke, the force of "Screw You," that is. For the insatiable *Star Wars* fans out there, this sound-effect-rich "Screwing" hits the spot. Actually, it is believed to have originated in the sound studio on the original *Star Wars* movie, NOT on the set. Rumor has it that while adding the sounds to the light-saber battle scenes the sound techs started using this sound (*voom . . . voom*) when they would flip each other off, which quickly transformed into role-playing light-saber battles with this sound. Nerdy, yet a huge part of popular culture. Thank you, Jedi masters!

Good times to use the Light Saber are:
     a. In line to see the next *Star Wars* movie.
     b. When you're dressed as a Jedi or Sith for Halloween.
     c. While watching *Star Wars* or even *Spaceballs* on DVD.

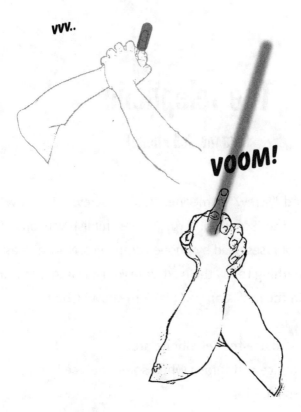

vvv..

VOOM!

Screw You How-To:

> Starting with both hands lowered in a fist, slowly raise the Bird on one hand and make the light-saber sound effect (*voom ... voom*) as if your Bird is the actual light saber, then continue to battle it out with your friend.

62

The Telephone

(aka the Cell Phone)

Reach out and "Screw" someone. Can I "Screw You" now? Good. Raising the "Screw You." Yup, all are childish versions of popular catchphrases used by phone companies. Now at least you have something to say the next time your call is lost or you get your bill in the mail. Can you thank me now? Good.

Good times to use the Telephone are:

    a. At a nice restaurant when someone's cell phone keeps ringing.

    b. If your friend loses his cell phone and you're helping him look for it. Lo and behold, you tell him to look: you found the "telephone."

    c. When your buddy is talking to his girlfriend on his cell phone.

Screw You How-To:

> Place your thumb to your ear and instead of extending
> your pinky toward your mouth, mimicking a phone, use
> your Bird. It also helps to mouth the words "Screw You."

[63]
The Hitchhiker

Fairly common, though it didn't come into existence until the emergence of the automobile.

Examples of when to use this are:

   a. While hitchhiking and a car or truck passes you and doesn't pick you up.
   b. While driving and you see a hitchhiker on the side of the road, roll down your window, slow down, and then flip him off and tell him to get a car.

Screw You How-To:

Use your thumb when hitchhiking, then switch to using
your Bird and turn it into the Classic Flip.

64

The Watch

When some poor schmuck asks you what time it is you can tell them it's time to buy a watch. Of course, turnabout is fair play, so expect the same kind of response if you're the schmuck who left his watch at home and needs to know the time.

Times to use the Watch are:

   a. When your friend just lost his watch.
   b. When the same guy keeps asking you what time it is.
   c. When your friends are running late.

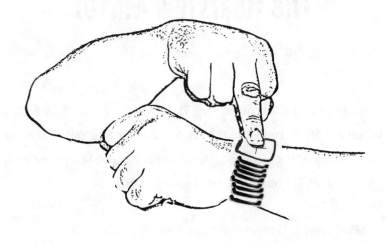

Screw You How-To:

Point to your wristwatch with your Bird.

65

The Rearview Mirror

Road rage is all the rage. Face it, we're surrounded by idiots when we drive. Even though we feel like getting out of the car and kicking some serious ass, because of state laws we can't. This may be the next best (and legal) thing.

Most useful times to use the Rearview Mirror are:
   a. When some jerk-off is blinding you from behind with his high beams.
   b. When another jerk-off is tailgating.
   c. When not only is a complete jackass tailgating you with his high beams on, but it's also snowing and blowing and you're just trying to concentrate on finding the road, which hasn't been plowed yet.

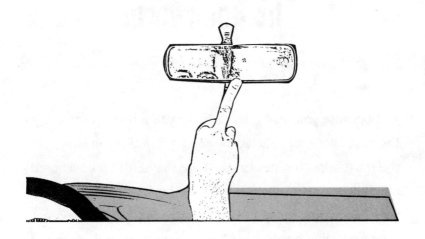

Screw You How-To:

When a car with an obnoxious driver is behind you and you can see him clearly in your rearview mirror, "adjust" your rearview mirror with your Bird.

[66]
The Bookworm

Just because you read doesn't make you a bookworm, but it's the best name for this "Screw You." After all, the people with the most opportunities to use it are the nerds who will pretty much be running the country in the next ten years or so anyway. Bookworm today, CEO tomorrow. But before they make their first million they have to pay their dues and endure the cruelty of high school bullies. Geeks, dweebs, nerds, losers, and dorks, this one's for you.

Good times to use the Bookworm are:
    a. While reading at a coffee shop and one of the jocks from school is in there with one of the cheerleaders drinking coffee.
    b. While reading at a job when you're supposed to be working, or at least look like you're working.

Screw You How-To:

> While reading a book, hold it up and open with your Bird on the outside spine of the book and the rest of your fingers curled on the outside with your thumb on the inside of the book for support.

67

The Pee-wee Herman

Yes, the same Pee-wee Herman from *Pee-wee's Playhouse*, the kids' show, who then graduated to another kind of show where he was arrested for indecent exposure. Anyway, before he was famous for doing something in public that everyone does in private, he was known to do a really messed-up dance where he'd point to his genitals. Go figure he'd be arrested for doing more than just pointing.

Times to use the Pee-wee Herman are:
  a. Ehh, actually never, unless your name happens to be Pee-wee Herman.
  b. If you really want to get your ass kicked.

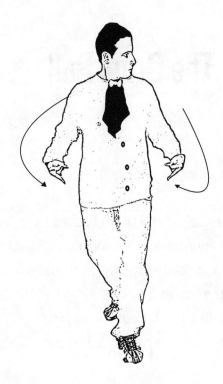

Screw You How-To:

Stand on your toes and use both Birds to point at your privates.

68

The Drum Roll

If you can carry a beat you can use this "Screw You."

The right times to use the Drum Roll are:

    a. When your friend is taking a dump in the bathroom and you're tapping on the door waiting to hear the splash.

    b. Just before you let out a loud fart.

    c. When you're waiting for someone to get ready.

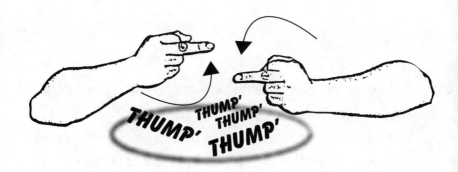

THUMP' THUMP' THUMP' THUMP' THUMP'

Screw You How-To:

Use your Birds as if they were drumsticks on any surface.

[69]
The Vulcan

Trekkies, this one's in your honor. Aside from going to *Star Trek* conventions dressed as Captain Kirk, Mr. Spock, or any other character on the show, what do you do to have fun? Well, we sure as hell don't know, you freaks. But we took the time to design a nice "Screw You" for you to use on the rest of the galaxy—and for those life-forms that might wish to reciprocate.

Lame-ass times to use the Vulcan are:

    a. If you're Leonard Nimoy and sick of all the freaky stalkers with pointy ears following you to the grocery store.

    b. At a *Star Trek* audition that you didn't get.

    c. When you see a bunch of Trekkies walking down the street.

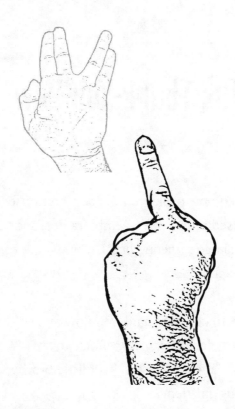

Screw You How-To:

> After you give the Vulcan sign (fingers in a V with a gap
> between the ring and Bird fingers) say, "Live long and . . ."
> and then turn the Vulcan sign into a Classic Flip and fin-
> ish with the words "Screw You."

[70]

The Thank-You Bow

Great for when you really pull a good one on one of your friends. It's used when you've embarrassed, shot down, put down, or humiliated someone, or otherwise made others laugh at their own expense.

Good times to use the Thank-You Bow are:
- **a.** Just before your victim starts to cry.
- **b.** You just embarrassed your little brother in front of his girlfriend.
- **c.** You just wiped out on your ass on the ice and everyone is laughing at you; try to save face.

Screw You How-To:

> With your right arm bent at the elbow in front of your
> stomach and your left arm bent at the elbow behind your
> back, bow. Both arms should be perpendicular to the floor
> with both Birds out.

Fill In the Blank

Based on Read Between the Lines. This one is pretty much the opposite of flipping the Bird. It's the absence of the Bird that makes this one stand out.

Good times to use this are:

a. Right after someone nailed you with Read Between the Lines, come right back with Fill In the Blank.

b. The next time you get a fill-in-the-blank pop quiz, say, "Fill *this* in."

c. When you get into an argument with someone and your mind is drawing a blank and you can't think of the right words to say.

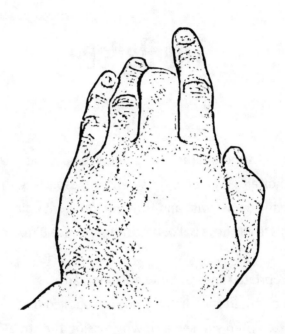

Screw You How-To:

Hold your hand out flat with fingers extended, but bring your Bird back into your palm so all other fingers are sticking up except the Bird. Now say, "Fill in the blank."

[72]
The Balloon

Similar to its more famous counterpart, Jazz, this "Screwer" is full of hot air. Everyone loves balloons, especially those cute ones that clowns twist and turn into different animal shapes. Well, this lovely little Balloon turns into a nice Bird.

Appropriate times to blow a Balloon are:

   a. When the birthday boy is a spoiled brat.
   b. When you see a clown crossing the street.
   c. When your boyfriend forgets your anniversary and tries to make it up to you by bringing you flowers. Tell him that was sweet and you'd like to give him something, too.

Screw You How-To:

> Put your thumb against your lips. With your hand in a fist
> start blowing onto your thumb and with each breath
> slowly raise your Bird till it becomes completely upright.

73

Two for Flinching

You know, sometimes just "Screwing" your friend isn't good enough. Sometimes you need to smack him around a little, too. Of course, if you do, make damn sure you don't do it to someone with a short fuse and a mean streak. Hundred for being stupid.

Examples of when to use this one are:
   a. He's just nailed you with a Bird.
   b. You just got hit with a snowball. So you run up to him really fast and flip him off.
   c. Everything is completely cool and calm at your friend's house. You're walking past him on the couch to go to the kitchen, and bam!

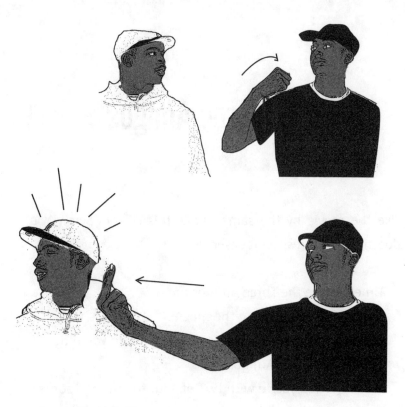

Screw You How-To:

> Quickly, as quickly as you can, and as close as you can, give the Bird to your friend's face. The faster you can give it to him and the closer you can get to his face without touching him, the better. You're looking for him to flinch. If he does, you say, "Two for flinching," and you get to punch him two times in the arm, hard.

74

The Three Amigos

Like the movie by the same name, this classic "Screw You" doesn't get the respect it deserves.

Times to use the Three Amigos are:
a. While watching the movie.
b. When at Don Pablo's restaurant and you order the Three Amigos.
c. When you're with two of your friends and some one asks who you are, say, "We are the Three Amigos."

Screw You How-To:

Fold your right arm across your chest, followed by your left arm across your chest. Next move both hands down to the sides of your hips, turn your head to the right, and instead of pushing your hips in, finish with a Classic Flip.

75

Come Here

(aka the Birdcall)

The call of the Bird. Unlike a lot of the ways of flipping the Bird, this one pulls people toward you instead of pushing them away. It's simple, straightforward, direct, AND effective.

Times and places to use Come Here are:

a. When you and your friend are on opposite sides of the bar and he wants you to come to him and you want him to come to you.

b. If you're an authority figure and you just caught some idiot doing something he's not supposed to. You need him to follow you.

c. When your friend is drunk and you need him to follow you out of the party so you can sober his drunk ass up.

Screw You How-To:

    Wave your Bird toward you when your target is a little distance away. Use the universal "come here" sign with your Bird rather than your index finger.

76

Lipstick

This one's made just for women—and cross-dressers. Every woman who wears lipstick knows how to blend it with her fingers once it's applied. Well, now there's a better way.

Times to use Lipstick are:
- a. In the women's bathroom when you're using the mirror along with twenty other women who are in your way.
- b. At a red light, when the guy in the car next to you is staring at you like he just got out of jail after twenty years.
- c. When your boyfriend is rushing you to get ready for going out.

Screw You How-To:

Blend the freshly applied lipstick with your Bird as you pucker up.

77

The Sign of the Cross

Don't get all religious here. This is to ward off vampires and Goths alike. The only bloodsucker this won't ward off is the IRS.

Appropriate times to use the Sign of the Cross are:

    a. When Goths are coming in your direction.

    b. When someone lets loose a fart that could wake the dead.

    c. When a guy you're talking to has garlic on his breath, or he just has bad body odor.

Screw You How-To:

Align both Birds at a 90-degree angle, forming a cross.

78

Itchy and Scratchy

Unfortunately, this one is not named after the cartoon on *The Simpsons*, just after one of life's little common annoyances.

   Times to use this are:
   a. HEL-*LO* . . . when you get an itch, stupid.
   b. Pretending you have an itch.
   c. Jock itch. (Also see the Screwball, #30.)

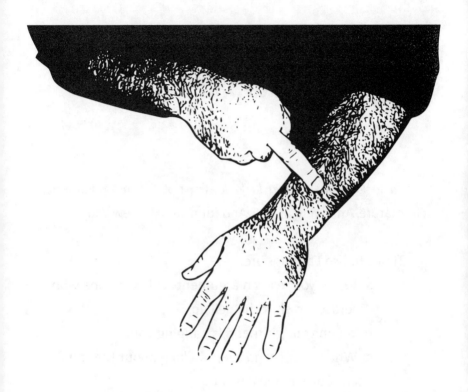

Screw You How-To:

When you have an itch, scratch it with your Bird.

[79]

Earplugs

La la la la la la la la la la la la. I'm not listening. Pathetic. Immature. Annoying as hell. And funny as a "Screw You!"

Times to use Earplugs are:

    a. When you're in an argument with someone who refuses to shut the hell up.

    b. When your girlfriend is nagging you.

    c. When your friend keeps talking about the same crap, day in and day out.

Screw You How-To:

Put a Bird in each ear and tell the person you're talking to that you're not listening.

80

Quotation Marks

This one is hilarious. Think Dr. Evil and Chris Farley. Used at the right time with the right amount of attention to how you say it, you can literally have one of your drunk friends pissing her pants laughing.

Times to use Quotation Marks are:
   a. While saying "Screw You" to someone.
   b. While saying something so obvious it's funny.
   c. While quoting a friend.

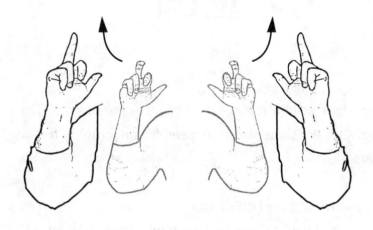

Screw You How-To:

Hold up both hands and use your Birds as imitation quotation marks above your head while you say something.

81

Dr. Evil

Don't look at him like he's friggin' Frankenstein, give him a hug. Cut him some slack, he's been frozen for thirty freaking years.

Fun times to use Dr. Evil are:
> a. If you're going to veterinary school. To be an evil vet.
> b. When you feel evil.
> c. If you're Robbie Knievel.

Screw You How-To:

Replace the famous Dr. Evil pinky-against-the-side-of-the-mouth with your Bird.

[82]
The Tie

Dressed to impress? Then you need a "Screw You" that's classy, sophisticated, stylish, and tasteful. This one is as close as you are going to get.

Times that call for the Tie are:
   a. When you end up seated next to someone you don't like at a wedding reception.
   b. When someone tells you to straighten out your tie at school.
   c. When you're getting dressed and you're pissed off because you can't for the love of God get your tie tied right.

Screw You How-To:

    While adjusting your tie, keep your Bird out.

[83]
The Premature Bird

Guys are familiar with this one. You know, jumping the gun, untimely release, a bit too excited, or just a wee bit early there, fella. We're talking about the Bird here and not your sex life, so *relax*. This premature shooter goes off when you see your target and impulsively give him the Bird before he has a chance to turn and face you to see it. So you've wasted it—again.

Times you might try to *avoid* use of this are:

a. If it's been a while since you've given a good "Screw" to someone and you're overanxious when you finally get the chance.

b. If you really don't care how your target feels because you do it for your own pleasure.

c. If you've really wanted to "Screw" this person for a long time and finally have the opportunity.

Screw You How-To:

You hurriedly give the Bird before your target can see it.

[84]
Missed!

From one extreme to the other.

Timing is everything when "Screwing" someone, and bad timing is, well, bad. Sometimes you only have one chance to "Screw" someone, so don't miss it. This Bird is all for naught, because you gave it and missed your shot.

Times you might have Missed! are:

    a. Someone flipped you off in the hallway while your hands were full of books.

    b. You tried to use the "Here, I've got something for you" Bird (#19) but your hand got stuck in your pocket.

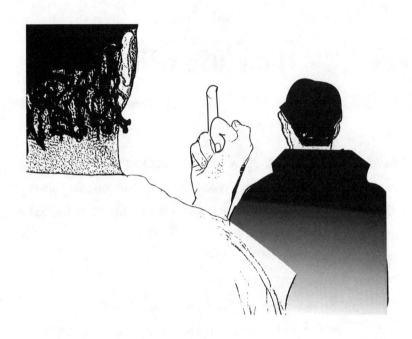

Screw You How-To:

Your target has given you the golden opportunity to "Screw" him and you hesitate and miss your chance. So you give the Bird to the wind.

85

The Close Call

We've all done things that we almost got caught doing. It's the way life is, full of close calls, what-ifs, and near misses. This is the "Screw You" that almost got you screwed up big time, but luckily it was just a close call.

Times that are Close Calls are:

    a. You're walking away from a friend with whom you've just been in an argument. You hear him call your name, and you turn around, about to give him the Bird—only to find that it was your teacher who called you.

    b. When a car behind you at night has its brights on as it's passing you. You turn to flip the driver off, but when you look over, you notice it's a police officer in an unmarked car.

Screw You How-To:

> Give someone the Bird just before he turns around to see you doing it; OR react instinctively to a situation by starting to give the Bird, only to come to your senses at the last second and refrain, saving you a world of trouble.

86

Oops

You've gone a little too far there, smart ass. Without thinking, you've gone and got yourself caught giving the Bird to someone you shouldn't have. Now prepare for the consequences.

Examples of Oops are:

    a. You try to use the Sneak Attack (#21) on your teacher and he catches you.

    b. A cop just gave you a ticket and he turns to go back to his car when you flip him off, only he turns again and sees you. Now you're the one who's "Screwed."

    c. You flip off someone you don't know who has a really short fuse and they come over and kick your ass.

Screw You How-To:

Give the Bird to someone you shouldn't.

87

The Mime

The white-faced, silent, scary-ass clown that pretends he's doing something with something that's invisible. Freaky. However, the mime does provide inspiration to this Bird. The sky's the limit with this one. If you can think it, and pretend to do it with something invisible, then you can give the Bird.

Examples of Mime times are:
   a. Pretending you're stuck in a box.
   b. Pretending you're playing Tug o' War.
   c. Pretending you're eating.

Screw You How-To:

Pretend you are doing something with an invisible object. Something like pretending you're stuck in a box and you use your hands to feel the inside of the box walls and press your face against it. Follow it up with flipping the Bird while your hands are against the invisible object.

88

The Gag

A great big thanks to supermodels for this one. Not only are they great to look at but they also make every teenage girl feel self-conscious and insecure about their looks to the point that a lot of them starve themselves to twigs or toss their cookies after every meal. Impossibly high standards, unrealistic goals, an unhealthy lifestyle, ahh, yes, living the American Dream.

Times to Gag are:

  a. Someone is dressed *sooo* badly that it makes you want to hurl.
  b. The couple sitting across the table from you is getting all huggy and kissy.

Screw You How-To:

Stick your Bird down your throat (or at least in your mouth) and make a gagging sound.

89

The Shadow Menace

Sometimes what is perceived is more powerful than what is real. Use this to its fullest when the opportunity presents itself to "Screw" with someone.

Best times to use the Shadow Menace are:

- a. In a classroom setting when a projector comes on and is casting white light on a screen.
- b. In a movie theater, if you are the projectionist or in the back row.
- c. When someone is lying down with their eyes closed, tanning, and you walk up to get their attention. Use the Bird to cast a shadow over their eyelids.

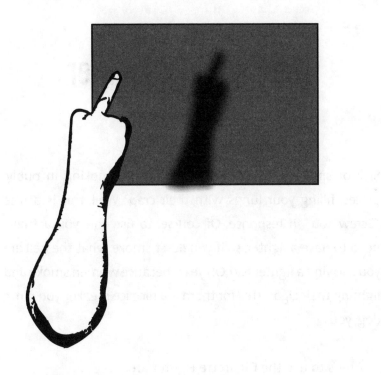

Screw You How-To:

Cast a shadow of your Bird against an object.

[90]
The Cigarette Lighter

Sick of smokers being inconsiderate and smoking in public places, filling your lungs with their crap? Well, this is a nice "Screw You" in response. Of course, to use this you actually need to have a lighter, so if you don't smoke what the hell are you carrying a lighter for? Oh yeah, because women smoke and lighting their cigarettes for them is a nice ice breaker, you pimp dog, you.

Times to use the Cigarette Lighter are:
   a. While lighting a friend's cigarette for him.
   b. You're a hot smoking chick and you want to light up while blowing off a guy who's staring at you.
   c. You're an inconsiderate bastard and light up after someone politely asks you not to smoke.

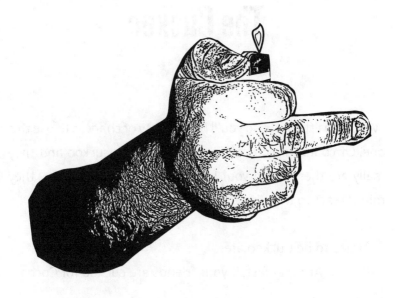

Screw You How-To:

When someone puts a cigarette to their mouth and is
searching for a light, pull out your lighter, keeping your
Bird straight out, and light a cigarette for the dirty
bastard.

[91]
The Cuckoo

We're all a little nuts, so you'll have plenty of chances to use this one. Of course, if you call someone crazy or cuckoo and they really are then watch your back, 'cause who knows how they might react to this Bird. But life is full of risks, so rock on!

Times to be Cuckoo are:
   a. At breakfast, if your friends are cuckoo for Cocoa Puffs.
   b. When someone you know does something really stupid in front of you and your buddies.
   c. While you're walking past a mental hospital.

Screw You How-To:

> The universal cuckoo signal is twirling your finger around
> your ear then pointing to someone that's nuts. Do it with
> your Bird instead of your index finger.

[92]
Hand Signals

If you took driver's ed. you know what hand signals are. If not, you're S.O.L. Inconsiderate drivers are the worst. They are the cause of road rage. They don't let you merge on the expressway, they don't let you out of a driveway at a red light, and they change lanes without signaling and then they cut you off. These pricks deserve a beating. We say, "Screw 'Em."

Times to use Hand Signals are:
- a. When coming to a STOP.
- b. When turning LEFT.
- c. When turning RIGHT.

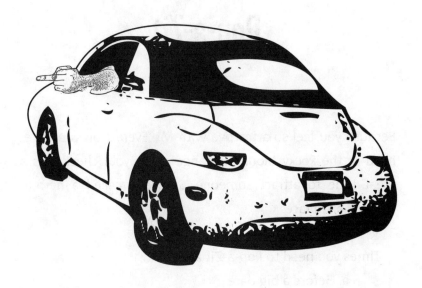

Screw You How-To:

> When getting in front of a rude driver, use your hand
> signals to indicate whether you are STOPPING, making
> a LEFT or making a RIGHT turn, and keep your Bird
> extended throughout.

*Warning: Driver Beware. People on the road don't take kindly to being
flipped off, no matter what they've done to provoke it.*

[93]
Pop-a-Zit

Because you feel so attractive with Mt. Everest on your forehead or the Rocky Mountain range down your cheeks, it's a great time to attract someone. Someone called a dermatologist, pizza face.

Times you need to Pop-a-Zit are:
  a. Before a big date.
  b. Before school pictures.
  c. When you're in the bathroom and feel like watching the white pus explode out all over the mirror.

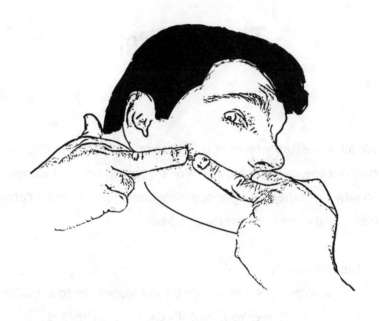

Screw You How-To:

Pop those ungodly whiteheads between your Birds.

94

The Lip Biter

We all make funny faces at one time or another, like when we stub our toe, are on the crapper, or are having sex, for example. So why not when we give someone the Bird? The most common facial expression for this is lip biting.

Times to use this are:

    a. When it's just a little bit inappropriate to actually say "Screw You," but it's OK to give the Bird.

    b. When it's really cold out and your lips are chapped.

    c. When you see someone mouth the words "Screw You" to you.

Screw You How-To:

    Bite your lower lip when giving the Bird. Bite lightly and expose your teeth during the expression.

95

The Big Dipper

Some people just look for a fight. If that's you, you're an ass-hole. But there *is* a "Screw You" that's right up your alley, tough guy. Sometimes flipping the Bird isn't enough to start trouble; to really push the issue you have to take extra measures. But beware! Someday you just might "Screw" with the wrong person and end up as a statistic.

Times you might use the Big Dipper are:

    a. In the lunchroom when you need to test your manliness by picking on the new kid in class at the table all by himself. (Hopefully he knows karate and kicks your stupid ass in front of the whole school.)

    b. You see something floating in someone's drink so you go and get it out for him.

Screw You How-To:

Flip the Bird and then proceed to turn it upside down and dip it in someone's drink.

96

Bring It On

Speaking of fights, this is another one that pushes buttons. When taunting goes too far, Bring It On.

Times to Bring It On are:
a. When a fight is inevitable so you get in one last "Screw You" before punches fly.
b. When your boxer is losing his fight and you're sure you could take the guy that's winning.
c. When you practice in front of a mirror to look tough.

Screw You How-To:

> Use both Birds as a way to signal to someone to come to
> you, by bending both your Birds and your wrists in a rapid
> motion toward you repeatedly.

97

The Typewriter

(aka the Keyboard)

This is one almost everyone has done, especially when learning how to type. Misspellings or sticking keys usually affect your anger level, and thus how hard you hit each key is based on how often you've "Screwed Up." Don't break a Bird on the board.

Times to use the Typewriter are:

a. When you're IMing and you're annoyed with the person you're talking to.

b. When typing an assignment that you had weeks to work on and didn't start until the very last minute and now you're cursing the person who assigned it to you because it's due tomorrow and it's already 3 a.m.

c. When you're text messaging someone with your cell phone rather than a keyboard.

Screw You How-To:

Instead of typing with your hands in the correct positions
(A-S-D-F, J-K-L-;), use each Bird to type one letter at a time.

[98]
The Stretch

Tired? Just waking up? Need to stretch your muscles? Or maybe you're just tired of all the morons in this world and you need to let them know you've had enough.

Times that call for a Stretch are:
a. At a baseball game during the seventh inning stretch, especially if you're on the Jumbotron.
b. When you're sitting next to your friend and it just feels right to stretch your arms out in front of his face, for the hell of it.
c. If you're a hot girl in tight shorts, and some guy behind you is staring at your butt when you're stretching at the gym.

Screw You How-To:

    However you decide to stretch, do it with your Birds
extended.

[99]
The Yawn

Bored? Can't stand the situation any longer because it's putting you to sleep and you're trying your hardest to stay up? Let the dullard know with an overly dramatic Yawn.

Yawn when:

    a. You're in class and your teacher is boring you about some lame-ass topic that you have absolutely no interest in whatsoever. That is why you'll be in summer school this year, again, and end up a lifelong McDonald's employee.

    b. You're on the phone listening to your girlfriend prattle on and on about her day and how she feels and where she thinks your relationship is going. You just want to watch the game with your friends, for crying out loud.

Screw You How-To:

Yawn and use your Bird to cover your mouth.

[100]
This Li'l Piggy

From those fun-filled days when you were a baby and Mommy used to play with your toes and make sounds like a wild animal (which might explain your sick fetishes), this one has history. To be used when all else fails.

Times to use this nursery rhyme are:
- a. NOT when you're babysitting your nephew.
- b. When your uncle is babysitting you.
- c. When you're high (on life).

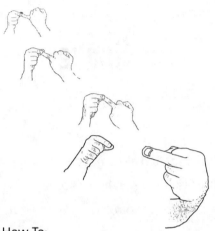

Screw You How-To:

Use your right index finger and thumb to hold the tip of your left pinky and shake it. Say, "This li'l piggy went to market."

Use your right index finger and thumb to hold the tip of your left ring finger and shake it. Say, "This li'l piggy stayed home."

Use your right index finger and thumb to hold the tip of your left Bird and shake it. Say, "This li'l piggy went . . ." Take your right hand away, just extend your Bird, and continue in that really irritating falsetto voice, "Screw You, Screw You, Screw You, all the way home."

[101]
The Shaker

Have you ever been so mad at someone or something that your body actually starts shaking? When you reach that point you're on the verge of one of two things: (1) passing out, or (2) giving a "Major Screwing Screw You." Sometimes both. Just remember what Van Wilder says—*You shouldn't take life too seriously. You'll never get out alive.*

Write that down.

Shake, rattle, and roll when:

    a. Your hometown football team just lost the Super Bowl on a last-second missed forty-seven-yard field-goal attempt.

    b. Your girlfriend just dumped you for your best friend.

    c. You just got fired.

Screw You How-To:

     Flip the Bird and scream at the top of your lungs, "SCREW YOOOOOOUUUUUUUUUUUUUUU!!!!!!!!!!!!!!" while shaking your Bird. Then pass out.

For more Birds

or to add your own,

go to

www.flipthebird101.com.

Acknowledgments

Whom do you thank in a book that's basically about flipping people off? People you care about or people you really would like to flip off? I'll take the high ground, if there is one, and thank the people who were positive influences in my life.

First and foremost, I'd like to thank the one person in my life whom I'll always try to emulate: my grandfather Frank Krakowiak (Gramps). He always had a smile on his face and a way about him that made others smile. It was his nature, his humor, his love. His whole life was dedicated to his grandsons, Rick and me. It's only appropriate that our first book recognize the tremendous impact he's had on our lives, and through us, the lives of the people we meet.

Of course to my parents, Virginia and Richard, thanks for instilling in me the values, morals, and love that it takes to make it in this world, both professionally and personally. I am the man I am today because of the child you loved, cherished, and raised for the past thirty-odd years. Thank you for being my parents; I couldn't have asked for better.

Thanks to my brother, Rick, who always encouraged me to do my best in everything. You never discouraged my creative and quite frankly off-the-wall sense of humor. I always took that to heart and wasn't afraid to say nine dumb ideas before the tenth one that turned out great. You taught me to take chances and believe in myself. Without that support, this book wouldn't have been written. Thank you.

To my friends growing up, the good and bad times we shared, I thank you for just being part of my life.

Thank you, Christian Lindner (CmyWork.com), for the wonderful illustrations in this book.

I'd also like to personally thank the people directly responsible for getting this book to print, starting with my amazing agent, Jonathan Close. Thanks for believing in me, and for taking a dream and making it a reality. Thanks also to agent Jake Ewell, for believing in this book and helping it become reality.

Thank you, Broadway Books, for publishing this book, especially to Becky Cole, not only for liking my book enough to green-light it, but for making the whole experience fun. Thank you. Also have to thank Brianne Ramagosa, for being there for me with the day-to-day communication and helping me get the little things done that I needed to do for the final version of the book–including reminding me to write these acknowledgments.

To everyone who reads this book, thanks for laughing.

Lastly, and certainly not least, thanks to everyone I've ever flipped the Bird to. Some in humor and some because you deserved it for cutting me off in traffic or for being a f***ing ass**** in general. This Bird's for you!

Go "Screw" Yourself.

Sincerely,

Jason Joseph

Jason Joseph

About the Authors

Born and raised in Buffalo, New York, **Jason Joseph** is a graduate of Medaille College, where he majored in media studies. This is his first book. He is currently single (and looking).

Rick Joseph, author, film producer, novelty toy manufacturer, and all-around creative guru, currently resides in Sherman Oaks, California, with his Shiba Inu, Kaimo. Originally from Buffalo, New York, Rick spent the last decade earning his stripes in the entertainment business as a producer, agent, manager, and studio executive. Rick has cut his comedy chops working with some of the brightest comedy minds in Hollywood and has been credited on such comedy classics as *Rush Hour* and *National Lampoon's Van Wilder*. Rick is currently a partner in Creative Hollywood Novelties LLC, a novelty toy manufacturer that creates humorous gifts for retail chains.